MOROCCAN

Colophon

© 2004 Rebo International b.v., Lisse, The Netherlands

www.rebo-publishers.com - info@rebo-publishers.com

Original recipes and photographs: © R&R Publishing Pty. Ltd.

Layout of inner pages: AdAm Studio, Prague, The Czech Republic

Cover design: Minkowsky Graphics, Enkhuizen, The Netherlands

ISBN 90 366 1618 2

MOROCCAN

the colors and fragrant spices of the souq for

creative cooking

REBO
PUBLISHERS

Foreword

Morocco is a mesmerizing country. A wander through its medieval medinas
or a visit to one of its magnificent palaces can take you centuries back in time.
Moroccan food is no less fascinating. Throughout Morocco, cooking is a part
of people's daily lives and the scent of amazing food rises from the street vendors'
stalls which fill the streets. The street is also the place to find many ingredients
and herbs, including cinnamon, cumin, saffron, Cayenne pepper, and paprika.
Cilantro is an essential ingredient of Moroccan cuisine.

Use this cookbook to bring a taste of Morocco to your own cooking. Follow any
of the 45 recipes and you will magically transform herbs, meat, fish, dried fruit,
and vegetables into typical Moroccan dishes. How do Lamb and Lentil Harira Soup,
Fish Tagine, and Herb Vegetable Couscous strike you? Or perhaps that Moroccan
specialty, Lambs' Brains in Tomato and Cilantro Sauce, is more to your liking!

Abbreviations

tbsp = tablespoon

tsp = teaspoon

oz = ounce

lb = pound

°F = degrees Fahrenheit

°C = degrees Celsius

g = gram

kg = kilogram

cm = centimeter

ml = mililiter

l = liter

qt = quart

All measurements conform to European
and American measurement systems.
For easier cooking, the American cup
measurement is used throughout the book.

Method

Place couscous in a microwave safe dish, add the water and salt and stand

3 minutes or until water is absorbed.

Dot the butter on top, cover with plastic wrap, leaving a small vent.

Microwave on high for 2 minutes. Stand until steam settles then lift off the wrap

and fluff up with a fork. Continue with recipe additions.

Quantity Calculation: Allow ¼ cup/56g of couscous per person.

Plain Steamed Couscous

Ingredients

Easy preparation: To each ½ cup/112.5 g of pre-cooked packet couscous, add:

½ cup/120 ml water

¼tsp salt

1tsp butter

moroccan

Method

Sift the flour, paprika and salt together into a large bowl. Make a deep well in the center and pour in ¼ of the measured mixture. Add the yeast and sugar, stir lightly to dissolve. Bubbles will appear to indicate that the yeast is active. Pour in the remaining water and the oil. With a wooden spoon, begin stirring from the center out, taking in flour gradually as you stir. Continue with your hand as it gets heavy, and form a dough.

Turn dough out onto a lightly floured surface (you may use white plain flour). Knead the dough for 8-10 minutes, sprinkling surface with a little flour if it sticks, until dough is smooth and elastic to touch.

Place in a clean, lightly oiled bowl, cover with plastic wrap and leave to rise in a warm place 30-40 minutes or until double its size.

With your fist punch the centre of the dough once, to release air, and turn out onto lightly floured surface. Knead for 2 minutes and then shape into an even log. Cut into 16 even pieces.

Roll out each piece into a 6 ½ cm/3 inch circle and place onto a kitchen towel in single layer; cover with another towel and leave to rise 15 minutes. Preheat the oven to 150°C/350°F.

Have ready a small plate sprinkled densely with sesame seeds, shake plate twice so seeds will be in single layer. Have beaten egg and brush ready and 2-3 lightly greased oven trays.

Ingredients

2 cups/450g stone ground wholemeal flour

¾tsp paprika

½tsp salt

1½ cups/330ml tepid water

sachet active dried yeast

(well within expiration date)

1tsp sugar

1tbsp olive oil

1 egg, lightly beaten to glaze

3 tablespoons or 1 packet sesame seeds

Moroccan Flat Breads

Brush 1 flat bread with a good coating of egg then lift and place bread egg side down onto the sesame seeds, press lightly and place in the oven, seed side up. Sprinkle the plate again with sesame seeds and repeat process. Continue with remainder. When first tray is full, place in oven and bake for 15 minutes and continue with remaining trays. It is best to cook 1 tray at a time on the center shelf. Place on cooling rack. May be stored in an airtight tin when cooled.

Note:

Ordinary wholemeal flour may also be used or use half white, half wholemeal.

Method

Mix all ingredients together thoroughly. Serve in a small bowl as a condiment or add about a teaspoonful to soups and stews.

Note: This version of harissa is quick and convenient. Store covered in the refrigerator. Refrigerate the jar of freshly chopped chilli after opening.

Will keep for many weeks.

Ingredients

1tbsp of chopped red chilli peppers from a jar of freshly chopped chilli

1 large clove garlic, crushed

1tsp ground cumin

½tsp ground coriander

1tbsp olive oil

Simple Harissa

Method

Place ingredients into an electric spice grinder or blender and grind finely.

Pass through a sieve, place the ground spice mix in a clean, screw top jar.

Use in tagines, rice and couscous stuffings, meat and chicken dishes. Use enough to taste or 1 or 2 teaspoons.

Ingredients

1tsp cumin seeds

1tsp coriander seeds

1½tsp black peppercorns

3 whole cloves

½ cinnamon stick

4 cardamom pods

2 pieces Mace bark

1tsp ground ginger

1tsp ground turmeric

Spice Blend (Ras el Hanout)

Although this quick method of preserving lemons departs from the traditional method, the result is the same.

Method

Wash lemons well, cut a slice from top and base to even off. Cut lemons in half lengthwise then cut each half into 4 wedges.

Place wedge side down on a board and cut off the white core (pith). With a sharp knife cut the flesh from the wedge down to the pith line and reserve.

Pack the wedge shaped skins lightly into a jar.

Remove the seeds from the lemon flesh and place the flesh into a food processor or blender bowl. Add the salt. Process until the lemon flesh is pulverised. Pour into the jar and cover the lemon rind.

Place the jar in the microwave and microwave on high power for 4 minutes. Remove the jar from the oven and when steam subsides screw on the lid. Shake or turn jar around to disperse juice and place in a dark cupboard.

After 3 days the lemon rind will be ready for use. The pith will look translucent and the preserved lemon will be soft to the bite. After opening, store in the refrigerator. To use: remove the amount needed, leaving the pulpy juice in the jar. Rinse the lemon well and cut into strips or dice as recipe instructs.

Note: This method allows you to make 2 to 3 lemons at a time. A jar (aproximately 1½ cup or 350 ml) will take 2 lemons filled to the top; 3 lemons need larger jar. If there is a space at the top, float a little oil on the surface before replacing the lid. Squeezed out lemon halves may be rinsed and added to the jar when room is available, but they will need time to mature.

Ingredients

3 good quality fresh lemons, at room temperature

3tbsp salt

Preserved Lemons

Method

Place the frozen beans in boiling salt water and cook about 10 minutes until tender. Drain, cool a little and then remove outer skin.

Toss the beans and onion together in a salad bowl. Whisk dressing ingredients together and pour over the salad. Toss well and chill before serving.

Broad Bean Salad with Cumin Dressing

Ingredients

2¼ cups/500g packet frozen broad beans

1 small Spanish onion, finely diced

1tsp ground cumin

2tbsp finely chopped Continental parsley

2 cloves garlic, finely chopped

salt to taste

freshly ground black pepper (optional)

Dressing

3tbsp olive oil

2tbsp lemon juice

Method

Heat olive oil, cumin seeds, fennel seeds, coriander seeds, cardamom, nutmeg and cinnamon in a saucepan over medium heat or about 2 minutes until fragrant.

Remove from heat, add olives and toss to coat. Stir in remaining ingredients. Refrigerate in an airtight container for at least 4 hours or up to 3 weeks.

Drain and serve at room temperature.

Ingredients

1 tbsp olive oil

1 tsp cumin seeds

1 tsp fennel seeds

1 tsp coriander seeds

¼ tsp cardamom, ground

pinch ground nutmeg

pinch cinnamon

1½ cups/337.5g green olives

1 tbsp lemon juice

1 tbsp orange juice

3 garlic cloves, minced

Moroccan Spiced Olives

Method

Wash the salad greens in cold water, drain and wrap in a clean kitchen towel. Place in the refrigerator for 1 hour or more to crisp.

Cut the skin from the oranges just past the pith line. Slice into ¼inch/½cm rounds crosswise. Remove stones and slice the dates lengthwise.

Arrange the salad greens on platter and top with circles of overlapping orange slices. Sprinkle with the dates and chopped walnuts.

Whisk dressing ingredients together and drizzle all over the salad.

Ingredients

1¾ cups/400g salad greens; eg mignonette,

coral or salad mix

3 medium sized oranges

3 ½tbsp fresh dates

3 ½tbsp walnut pieces, coarsely chopped

Dressing

2tbsp lemon juice

½tsp sugar

2tbsp light salad oil

salt, freshly ground black pepper to taste

Orange Date and Walnut Salad

moroccan

Method

Peel the lemons removing the pith. Cut in half lengthwise, removing the core and seeds and cut into ¼inch/½cm dice.

Toss the lemon, onion, parsley and sugar together. Add salt to taste, place in serving bowl. Sprinkle lightly with ground black pepper. Serve with other appetizers or to accompany seafood dishes.

Ingredients

3-4 fresh thin skinned lemons

1 large Spanish onion, diced

¾cup/170g coarsely chopped

Continental parsley

½tsp sugar (optional)

salt to taste

freshly ground black pepper

Diced Lemon and Onion Salad

Method

Peel the oranges with a sharp knife, removing all pith. Remove segments by cutting through the membrane on each side of the segment. Release the segment.

Trim top and root end of the radishes and grate on a coarse grater.

Toss the orange segments and grated radish together in a salad bowl.

Mix the lemon juice, sugar and salt together and pour over the salad. Toss gently. Chill before serving.

Radish and Orange Salad

Ingredients

4 oranges

10 red radishes, washed well

½cup/100ml fresh lemon juice

1tbsp sugar

pinch of salt

Method

Drain the soaked beans and remove the skins. Place in a large saucepan with the water, garlic and onion. Bring to the boil and boil at a steady pace for 40 minutes or more until the beans are very soft. The time varies with different batches of beans. Skim off any froth as it rises to the surface, add extra water if needed.

Place the beans, garlic, onion and some of the cooking water in a food processor and puree until smooth, adding extra liquid when needed.

Return the puree to a clean saucepan, place over low heat, stir in the salt to taste, olive oil and spices, and continue to cook until smooth and heated through. Add more cooking liquid to make a soft consistency.

Pour into individual soup bowls and garnish with a ribbon of paprika and one of chives diagonally across the surface. Serve with Moroccan bread (Page 000) and vegetable sticks and small jugs of olive oil and lemon juice to be added at will.

Ingredients

2¼ cups/500g dried broad beans, soaked overnight

2½ pint/1½l water or to cover

4 large cloves garlic

1 onion, diced

salt to taste

½ cup/120 ml virgin olive oil

2tsp ground cumin

2tsp paprika

Garnish

paprika

finely chopped chives

Bessara

To Serve

Moroccan bread and vegetable sticks

Method

Place the chicken pieces in a large saucepan and add the next 9 ingredients. Pour in 3 cups/720 ml of water, bring to the boil, reduce heat, cover and simmer gently for 45-50 minutes until chicken is tender.

With slotted spoon, place chicken on plate. Cool and then remove the bones and discard. Cut chicken meat into small pieces and return to saucepan.

Add remaining 5 cups/1½ liters of water and bring back to a simmer. Stir constantly as the couscous is slowly added to distribute evenly. Add the mint, parsley and coriander. Simmer uncovered for 10 minutes, stirring occasionally. Add lemon juice, adjust seasoning if needed and serve immediately.

Ingredients

3½ cups/750g chicken casserole pieces

2 cups/420g can diced tomatoes

1 onion coarsely grated

½tsp cumin

½tsp paprika

½tsp turmeric

⅛tsp cayenne pepper or chilli powder

1 cinnamon stick

1 small clove garlic, crushed

salt and freshly ground black pepper to taste

8 cups/2 liters water

½ cup/112.5g couscous

3tbsp chopped mint

2tbsp chopped Continental parsley

2tbsp chopped coriander

2tsp lemon juice or to taste

Chicken and Couscous Soup (Shurba Suksu)

Method

Saute onion, celery, garlic and pepper until softened. Add cinnamon, ginger and turmeric.

Stirring thoroughly, add stock and lentils and bring to a boil. Reduce heat, cover and simmer for 45 minutes.

Add chickpeas and tomatoes and cook for another 15 minutes. Stir in lemon juice, coriander and salt and pepper (to taste). Serve immediately.

Moroccan Chickpea Lentil Soup

Ingredients

1 medium onion, sliced

3 cloves garlic, crushed

1 red capsicum, diced

2 stalks celery, chopped

2tsp olive oil

½tsp cinnamon

½tsp ginger

½tsp turmeric

6 cups/1440 ml chicken or vegetable stock

1⅓ cups/330g lentils, rinsed

4 cups/80g chickpeas

2 cups/400g tomato pieces

½ cup coriander, finely chopped

¼ cup/60 ml lemon juice

salt and pepper, to taste

moroccan

Method

Heat the oil in a large pot, add the onion and cook over a medium heat for 3 minutes, or until the onion is soft and golden.

Add the spices and chilli and cook about 2 minutes until fragrant.

Stir in the tomatoes, chickpeas and fish stock and bring to a boil.

Reduce the heat and simmer uncovered for 15 minutes.

Add the fish and cook for 5 minutes, or just until the fish is tender.

Remove the soup from the heat and then add the couscous and cover. Set aside for 10 minutes or until the couscous is soft.

Serve with a dollop of yoghurt and sprinkle with parsley and mint.

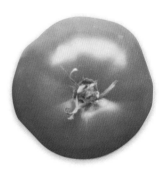

Ingredients

1 tbsp olive oil

1 onion, chopped

1 tsp ground coriander

1 tsp ground cumin

1 tsp allspice

1 green chilli, finely sliced

2 cups/400 g chopped tomatoes

2 cups/400 g chickpeas, rinsed and drained

1 liter reduced salt fish stock

2 cups/500 g firm white fish fillets (redfish, bream, sea perch), cut into large pieces

⅓ cup/75 g couscous

thick, reduced fat natural yoghurt, to serve

1 tbsp chopped fresh parsley

1 tbsp chopped fresh mint

Spiced Fish, Tomato and Chickpea Soup

Method

In a large saucepan, melt the butter and stir in the cinnamon, ginger, turmeric, paprika, pepper and saffron threads. Cook slowly for 2 minutes until aromatic.

Add the diced lamb and onion. Stir to coat with spices. Stir in parsley, coriander, tomatoes, water and chickpeas. Bring to the boil then turn down and simmer for 1 hour.

Add the lentils and cook a further 45 minutes until the lentils are soft. Add lemon juice and salt and cook 5 minutes. Serve with lemon slices and extra parsley if desired.

Ingredients

2tbsp butter

1½tsp cinnamon

1tsp ground ginger

1tsp turmeric

1tsp paprika

½tsp black pepper

pinch saffron threads

2 cups/500 g diced lamb

1 large onion, finely chopped

⅓ cup/75g chopped continental parsley

⅓ cup/75g chopped coriander

2 cups/400g can tomatoes, diced

5-6 cups/1½ –2 liters water

2 cups/410g chickpeas, drained and rinsed

½ cup/125g lentils, washed

2tbsp lemon juice

salt to taste

lemon slices and extra chopped parsley, to serve

(optional)

Moroccan Harira

Method

Heat a small heavy-based saucepan, add the almond meal and stir quickly until lightly toasted. Remove from heat and stir until aroma arises. Remove to a bowl immediately to prevent further coloration. Add the remaining paste ingredients and blend to make a thick spreadable paste, adding extra drop of juice if needed.

Cut into the side of the fish fillet to form a pocket. Lightly sprinkle top and inside pocket with salt. Divide the almond paste into 4 portions. Spoon ½ a portion into the pocket and press to close. With fingers press the other half on top in a neat layer. Make score marks on top with a fork.

Brush a suitable ovenproof serving dish with melted butter, spread in the diced onion, sprinkle on the saffron and pepper. Set the fish fillets on top of the onion and pour the water in down the side. Drizzle the fish with the remaining melted butter.

Bake in a preheated oven 180°C/350°F for 20-25 minutes until cooked.

Serve immediately with salad accompaniment.

Baked Fish with Almond and Orange Paste (Hut Benoua)

Ingredients

Almond Paste

1 cup/200g packet almond meal (ground almonds)

1tbsp unsalted butter, softened

⅓ cup/75g icing sugar

3tsp ground cinnamon

1tbsp fresh orange juice

Fish

4 white fish fillets, centre cut, ¾in/1½cm thick (egling, gemfish, schnappers)

salt to taste

3tbsp unsalted butter, melted

1 large onion, diced

⅛tsp powdered saffron

¼tsp black pepper

⅓ cup/80ml water

Method

Combine the first 5 ingredients and rub into both sides of the fish cutlets. Place on plate, cover and refrigerate 2 hours for flavor to penetrate.

Heat oil in a large frying pan and sear the fish on both sides until lightly colored. Remove immediately and set aside.

Add the diced onion to the pan, adding reserved oil if needed. Fry gently while stirring until soft. Stir in pepper and cinnamon, honey, vinegar, raisins and parsley. Turn heat to low and simmer for 10 minutes. Return the fish to the pan, spoon some sauce over the fish, cover and simmer 10 minutes, basting occasionally with sauce. Serve immediately with rice or couscous.

Fish Tagine with Raisins and Honey

Ingredients

1tbsp olive oil

¼tsp ground cumin

¼tsp ground cinnamon

¼tsp cayenne pepper

¼tsp powdered saffron

4 fish cutlets

2tbsp olive oil

1 large Spanish onion, finely diced

2tbsp finely chopped continental parsley

¼tsp each ground black pepper and cinnamon

4tbsp honey

4tbsp wine vinegar

¾ cup/169g raisins, soaked and drained

Method

Cut the fish into ¾ inch/2 cm cubes and place into a large, non-metallic dish. Grate the onion into a bowl, add the garlic, spices, oil, lemon juice and salt. Mix well and pour over the fish, turning fish to coat all sides. Cover and marinate 1 hour or more in the refrigerator. Soak bamboo skewers.

Prepare the Chermoula. Heat the 3 spices in a small pan about 30 seconds or until fragrant. Combine with the garlic, oil and lemon juice and whisk well until thick. Stir in the parsley, coriander and onion. Set aside.

Thread the fish cubes onto 4-5 skewers. Grill under hot grill bars or on oiled grill plate or barbeque. Serve on a bed of saffron rice with the chermoula drizzled over the fish.

Marinated Fish Skewers with Chermoula

Ingredients

750g/1½lb thick white fish steaks, eg ling, gemfish

1 small onion, grated

1 clove garlic, crushed

1 tsp paprika

½tsp cumin

3tbsp olive oil

2tbsp lemon juice

½tsp salt

Chermoula

½tsp ground coriander

2tsp cumin

1tsp paprika

3 cloves garlic, crushed

⅓ cup/80ml olive oil

¼ cup/60ml lemon juice

½ cup/112.5g chopped fresh coriander

1 small Spanish onion, finely chopped (optional)

Method

Flake the crab meat and remove any sinew. Shell the prawns and cut into small pieces.

Heat oil in a frying pan, sauté the onions and garlic for 1 minute, add the next 4 spices and stir quickly until aromatic. Stir in the diced tomato, cook a little and then add the chopped prawns. Cook until they turn pinkish. Mix in the coriander and breadcrumbs and combine well. Remove from heat and set aside.

To roll: Place 6 strips on work surface and lightly spray or brush with oil. Double up, combining the 6 into 3 strips.

Place a tablespoon of mixture on the end and sides of each double strip 2cm/¾ inch. Lift end piece over filling. Turn in the side strips all the way up, brush strips and top end lightly with water and roll to the end. Place seam side down on a greased oven tray and spray or brush lightly with oil. Repeat, making 3 rolls at a time until all are completed.

Preheat oven to 180°C/350°F and bake for 20-25 minutes until golden and crisp. Serve hot.

Ingredients

½ cup/125g can crab meat

1 cup/200g medium size green prawns

1½tbsp olive oil

1 small onion finely chopped

2 cloves garlic, crushed

½tsp cumin

½tsp paprika

¼tsp powdered saffron

pinch of cayenne pepper

1 large tomato, skinned, seeded and diced

¼ cup/56g finely chopped fresh coriander

¼ cup/56g fresh breadcrumbs

2 cups/375g packet filo pastry

olive oil for brushing or use oil spray

Seafood Rolls (Briouts)

Method

Soak 4 wooden skewers in water for at least 10 minutes. Toss the chicken with the oil, garlic, ground spices, cayenne, salt and 1 tablespoon of lemon juice until the pieces are evenly coated.

Preheat the grill to high. Thread the chicken onto the skewers and grill for 8-10 minutes, turning occasionally, until slightly charred, cooked through and tender. Keep warm.

Meanwhile, prepare the couscous according to the packet instructions, then fluff it with a fork. Stir the butter, remaining lemon juice, coriander and olives into the couscous and season. Transfer to serving plates, top with the chicken and drizzle any pan juices over the whole. Serve with the lemon wedges and garnish with coriander.

Ingredients

4 large skinless boneless chicken breasts, cut into 2.5cm (1in) cubes

1tbsp olive oil

1 clove garlic, crushed

1tsp each of ground coriander, ginger and cinnamon

Pinch of cayenne pepper

¼tsp salt

Juice of 1½ lemons

1 cup/250g couscous

2 tbsp butter

2 tbsp chopped fresh coriander, plus extra leaves to garnish

½ cup/100g pitted black olives, chopped

Black pepper

Lemon wedges to serve

Chicken with Lemon and Coriander
Couscous

Method

Combine cumin, cayenne, parsley and oregano. Rub spices evenly into pork and thread onto skewers.

Lightly brush skewers with oil before and during cooking. Cook on lightly oiled BBQ or grill on medium-high heat for 5-6 minutes (turn 2-3 times) or until juices run and meat colors just pink to clear when pierced with a skewer.

Allow pork to rest for a few minutes before serving.

Serve with almond, apricot and coriander couscous.

Ingredients

1lb/500g lean diced pork pieces (1in/2cm x 1in/2cm cubes)

1tbsp ground cumin

¼tsp cayenne pepper

1tsp dried parsley flakes

1tsp dried oregano flakes

2tbsp olive oil

Cumin Spiced Pork Kebabs

moroccan

Method

Flatten the chicken fillets to an even thickness with a meat mallet. Mix marinade ingredients together and rub well into the chicken on both sides with your fingers. Place in a flat, non-metallic dish, pour any remaining marinade over the mixture, cover and marinate for 2 hours, or more if refrigerated.

Just prior to cooking, mix the chermoula ingredients together in a bowl. Toss well to distribute ingredients.

Heat barbeque or chargrill plate to moderate or high heat, oil the bars and grill the chicken for 3-4 minutes each side, depending on thickness; brush with any reserved marinade as they cook.

Prepare serving platter or individual plates with a bed of French fries or rice. Place chicken on top. Spoon chermoula neatly on top of each fillet. Garnish with black olives and preserved lemon. Serve immediately.

Note: Cover grill bars with a sheet of baking paper for a good result. May also be grilled in a heated, heavy-based frying pan lined with baking paper.

Chargrilled Chicken with Mint Chermoula

Ingredients

4 chicken breast fillets

Marinade

½tsp ground ginger

½tsp turmeric

½tsp dried mint

½tsp salt

1tbsp lemon juice

1tbsp olive oil

Mint Chermoula

½ cup/112.5g chopped fresh mint

2tbsp very finely chopped Spanish onion

1tsp finely chopped preserved lemon

2tsp finely chopped black olives (optional)

1tbsp olive oil

1tbsp lemon juice

salt, black pepper to taste

Garnish

4 black pitted olives, halved

preserved lemon cut into fine strips

French fries or steamed rice to serve

moroccan

49

Method

Combine all kefta ingredients together in a large bowl. Knead by hand for 3-4 minutes to make a fine texture. Take a good tablespoon of mixture and roll into a ball with wet hands. Repeat process, placing in single layer on a tray, cover and refrigerate.

Heat oil in a large frying pan, add a few meatballs at a time and roll around the pan to sear on all sides. Remove and repeat with remainder.

Prepare the sauce, heating oil in a large saucepan and gently frying the onion until soft and golden. Add the garlic and spices and cook for 30 seconds, stirring, until fragrant. Stir in the diced tomatoes, water, harissa OR chilli flakes and parsley. Bring to the boil.

Add the meat balls, return to a boil; then turn heat down. Simmer gently for 50 minutes. Add the coriander and simmer 5 minutes. Adjust seasoning and serve with rice, couscous or Moroccan bread (page 8-9).

Lamb Kefta in Tomato Sauce (Kefta Ghan' Mi Bel')

Ingredients	Tomato Sauce
Kefta	1tbsp olive oil; 1 onion, finely chopped
2lb/1kg minced lamb; 1 onion, finely chopped	2 cloves garlic, crushed
2 cloves garlic, crushed	2tsp cumin; 1 tsp paprika
½tsp ground ginger	½tsp ground cinnamon
½tsp ground cardamom	1¾ cups/2400g cans diced tomatoes
1tsp cumin; 1 tsp paprika	½ cup/120ml water
2tbsp finely chopped continental parsley	1tsp harissa (page 10-11) or
2tbsp finely chopped fresh coriander	½tsp dried chilli flakes
2tbsp dried breadcrumbs	¼ cup/56g chopped fresh coriander
salt, pepper to taste	¼ cup/56g chopped fresh continental parsley

Method

Combine all the ingredients for the meatballs and form into 1 inch/2cm balls with wet hands. Heat a large, heavy based saucepan or casserole dish and add the olive oil. Brown the meatballs in the oil, then remove, leaving the oil in the pot. Set the meatballs aside, covered.

Add the garlic, onion, and capsicum to the reserved oil and sauté until the onion is clear. Add the remaining ingredients for the sauce and simmer, covered, 30 minutes until the sauce has cooked down to a thick gravy.

Return the meatballs to the sauce and simmer uncovered for 10 minutes more. Carefully bread the eggs into the sauce and poach for a few minutes (don't overcook the eggs.) Serve at once.

Meatball Stew

Ingredients

Meatballs

1lb/500g lamb mince

2tbsp chopped parsley

1tbsp chopped fresh coriander

½tsp ground cumin

½ onion, peeled and finely chopped

¼tsp cayenne

salt to taste

2tbsp olive oil for pan frying

2 cloves garlic, peeled

2 medium onions, peeled and finely chopped

1 green capsicum, cored, seeded and chopped

1 small bunch of parsley, chopped

2lb/1kg tomatoes, chopped

1tsp ground cumin

1tsp freshly ground black pepper

½tsp ground cinnamon

2tbsp fresh lemon juice

¼tsp cayenne

1½tsp salt (or to taste)

6 eggs

Method

Soak brains in cold water for 30 minutes and then carefully remove the fine membrane cover. Separate the 2 lobes, then soak again in lightly salted cold water to remove all traces of blood. Rinse under running water.

Heat the oil in a large frying pan, add the crushed garlic and lightly sauté. Stir in the diced tomatoes, sugar, paprika, ginger, salt and pepper and simmer for 3 minutes stirring occasionally. (Add the lemon juice)

Add the brains, ladle some sauce on top, cover and simmer for 5 minutes. Turn brains over and continue to simmer 2 minutes more.

When brains are firm, cut each lobe in half, stir in the coriander and simmer 3 minutes more until solidified, or thickened. Adjust seasoning. Transfer to a serving dish, cover and refrigerate to cool. Serve cold as an appetizer.

Ingredients

6 sets lambs' brains

3tbsp olive oil

3 cloves garlic, crushed

1lb/500g ripe firm tomatoes, skinned, seeded and diced

1tsp sugar

1tsp paprika

1½tsp ground ginger

½tsp salt

freshly ground black pepper to taste

juice of ½ a lemon

½ cup/112.5g finely chopped coriander leaves

Brains in Coriander and Tomato
Sauce (Moukh M'Charmel)

Method

Heat the oil in a large saucepan or frying pan with a lid and brown the chicken pieces, a few at a time. Remove to a plate. Add remaining oil and sliced onions and cook gently until soft and slightly golden. Drain some of the oil from the pan if you wish.

Add spices and stir a few seconds. Return chicken pieces to the pan, turn and coat well with the spices. Add the chicken stock, chick peas, lemon juice and pepper. Bring to a boil, then reduce heat and simmer covered for 40 minutes.

Add the parsley and coriander and simmer 10-15 minutes more until chicken is very tender and sauce is reduced.

Remove to a serving dish or platter, sprinkle lightly with chopped parsley and serve with Moroccan flat bread.

Moroccan Chicken with Chickpeas (Ferakh bi Hummus)

Ingredients

3tbsp olive oil

3lb/1½kg whole chicken, cut into serving pieces, or purchase ready-cut pieces

1 large Spanish onion, thinly sliced

1tsp turmeric

¼ tsp paprika

½tsp salt

cups chicken stock

2 cups/400g can chick peas, drained, rinsed and skins removed

juice of 1 lemon or to your liking

freshly ground black pepper

Method

Heat the oil in a frying pan, add the onion and clove of crushed garlic and cook over a medium heat for 1 minute. Add the lamb and cook until the lamb is browned, breaking the meat up with a fork. Drain any excess oil from the pan. Add the tomatoes, cumin, ground cilantro and cinnamon and cook for 5 minutes. Stir in the fresh cilantro and 2 teaspoons lemon juice.

Preheat the oven to 400°F/200°C. Spread the lamb topping over the pizza bases and sprinkle with the pine nuts and mozzarella. Bake for 10 minutes or until the cheese has melted and the pizzas are heated through.

To make the raita, mix the yogurt, grated cucumber, crushed clove of garlic and chopped mint in a bowl.

Toss the mint and parsley leaves in the remaining lemon juice and season with pepper. Serve the pizzas topped with the herb leaves, raita and relish.

Ingredients

1tbsp sunflower oil

1 red onion, finely chopped

1 clove garlic, crushed

½lb/225g lean ground lamb

½ cup/112.5g canned crushed tomatoes

1tsp ground cumin

1tsp ground coriander

½tsp cinnamon

1tbsp chopped fresh cilantro

1tbsp lemon juice

4 single-serve pizza bases

2tbsp pine nuts, toasted

½ cup/125g reduced-fat mozzarella cheese, grated

1 cup/225g fresh mint leaves

1 cup/225g fresh Italian parsley

cracked black pepper

2tbsp mango relish

Moroccan Lamb Pizza

Raita Yogurt Relish

1 cup/240ml reduced-fat natural

yogurt

1 Lebanese cucumber, grated

1 clove garlic, crushed

1 tbsp fresh mint, chopped

Method

Marinade:

Place parsley, rosemary, thyme, garlic, black pepper, lemon juice and zest and oil in a non-reactive bowl. Add chicken. Toss to combine. Cover. Marinate in the refrigerator for at least 30 minutes.

Preheat barbecue or grill to a high heat. If using bamboo skewers, soak in cold water for at least 20 minutes.

Thread chicken onto skewers. Place on barbecue grill or under grill.

Cook, brushing frequently with marinade and turning, for 6-10 minutes or until chicken is cooked. Serve with Red Bell Pepper Harissa for dipping.

Red Bell Pepper Harissa

Preheat the grill to hot. Using your hands, flatten pepper and tomato halves and place skin side up on foil under grill. Cook until skins blacken. When cool, remove skins.

Place the pepper and tomato flesh in a food processor and add other ingredients to taste. Purée.

Set aside until ready to serve.

Ingredients

455g/1lb skinless chicken breast fillets, trimmed of visible fat, cut into ¾in/2cm cubes

1 quantity Red Bell Pepper Harissa optional

Moroccan Lemon Marinade

1tbsp chopped fresh parsley

1tbsp fresh rosemary leaves or 2 tsp dried rosemary

2tsp fresh thyme or 1 tsp dried thyme

1 clove garlic, crushed

1tsp crushed black peppercorns

grated zest and juice of 1 lemon or 1 preserved lemon

1tbsp olive oil

Moroccan Lemon Chicken Shish Kebabs

Red Bell Pepper Harissa

2 red bell peppers, cut in half lengthwise, seeds removed

1 plum tomato, cut in half lengthwise, seeds removed

1 tsp red wine vinegar

2 tsp tomato paste

hot chili sauce

freshly ground black pepper

moroccan

Method

Mix the garlic, spices, seasonings and lemon juice together. Rub the drumsticks well with the mixture by hand, place in non-metallic containers, stand to marinate for 2 hours or longer if refrigerated.

Heat oil and butter in a wide based saucepan or lidded skillet. Dust each drumstick with flour. Place in the pan a few at a time and turn to brown on all sides. Add the onion, preserved lemon, stock powder and about 2-2 ½ cups of water to just cover the chicken.

Cut the skinned tomatoes in halves crosswise and squeeze out the seeds. Place the halves over the chicken and sprinkle in the coriander. Bring to a boil, then turn down and simmer for 1 hour. After 40 minutes, add the olives.

Lift drumsticks onto a heated serving platter, cover and keep hot. Place any large pieces of cooked tomato on top; then boil the remaining sauce, uncover until thickened and pour over the chicken. Sprinkle with finely chopped parsley and serve immediately with Moroccan bread.

Spiced Chicken Drumsticks with Tomato-Coriander

Ingredients

2 cloves garlic, crushed

¼tsp powdered saffron

¼tsp cumin

¼tsp paprika

pinch cayenne pepper

onion

½tsp salt

freshly ground black pepper

2tbsp lemon juice

12 chicken drumsticks

flour for dusting

2tbsp olive oil

2tbsp butter

8 preserved lemon segments (page 000)

water to cover

1½tsp chicken stock powder

3 large ripe tomatoes, skinned, halved and seeded

2tbsp finely chopped coriander

10 black olives

1tbsp finely chopped parsley

Method

Combine cumin, cayenne, parsley and oregano. Rub spices evenly into pork and thread onto skewers.

Lightly brush skewers with oil before and during cooking. Cook on lightly oiled BBQ or grill on medium-high heat for 5-6 minutes (turn 2-3 times) or until juices run and meat colors just pink to clear when pierced with a skewer.

Allow pork to rest for a few minutes before serving.

Serve with almond, apricot and coriander couscous.

Ingredients

1lb/500g lean diced pork pieces (1in/2cm x 1in/2cm cubes)

1tbsp ground cumin

¼tsp cayenne pepper

1tsp dried parsley flakes

1tsp dried oregano flakes

2tbsp olive oil

Cumin Spiced Pork Kebabs

moroccan

Method

To make the marinade, place the garlic, yogurt, oil, cumin, coriander, paprika, cayenne and lemon juice in a large non-metallic bowl and mix well. Add the lamb, turning to coat. Cover and place in the fridge for 1 hour to marinate. If using wooden skewers, place them in water to soak for 10 minutes.

Stir the apricots and mint into the lamb and season. Thread the meat and apricots onto 8 metal or wooden skewers, placing a lemon wedge at both ends. Discard the marinade.

Preheat the grill to high. Place the kebabs on a baking sheet under the grill and cook for 8-10 minutes, turning occasionally, until the meat has browned. Spoon the juices over all and serve.

Spiced Lamb and Apricot Kebabs

Ingredients

1lb/500g lamb leg steaks, cut into

1in/2.5cm pieces

½ cups/125g ready-to-eat dried apricots

1tbsp finely chopped fresh mint

Salt and black pepper

1 lemon, cut into 8 wedges

For the marinade

1 clove garlic, crushed

2tbsp low-fat natural yogurt

1tbsp olive oil

1tsp ground cumin

1tsp ground coriander

1tsp paprika

Pinch of cayenne pepper

Juice of 1 lemon

Method

Slice off the 4 sides of the capsicum, trim off curved ends so pieces are flat. Brush or spray the skin side with oil. Grill under a hot grill skin side up, until skin has blistered. Remove to a plastic bag, stand 15 minutes to sweat.

Remove stems from the eggplant. Peel off ½inch/1cm wide strips of skin lengthwise at intervals for a striped effect. Slice into rounds ½cm/¼inch thick. Set aside.

Brush or spray both sides of the eggplant with oil. Grill on both sides until rosy, browned and cooked through. Place attractively onto a serving platter.

Skin the capsicum slices and cut into small dice. Sprinkle over the eggplant.

Whisk the dressing ingredients together and pour over the eggplants.

Stand 10 minutes before serving.

Eggplant and Red Pepper Salad

Ingredients

4 medium sized eggplants, washed

1 red capsicum

¼ cup/60ml olive oil or oil spray

Dressing

3tbsp olive oil

2tbsp lemon juice or vinegar

2 cloves garlic, crushed

½tsp paprika

¼tsp cayenne pepper

2tbsp finely chopped flat leaf parsley

moroccan

Method

Heat oil in a saucepan over a medium heat, add ginger, cinnamon, cumin seeds and tumeric and cook, stirring, for 1 minute. Add onions and cook for 3 minutes longer or until onions are soft.

Add red kidney beans, soy beans, chickpeas, chicken (if using), tomato paste and stock to pan and bring to the boil. Reduce heat and simmer for 10 minutes.

Add currants and pinenuts and cook for 2 minutes longer.

Ingredients

1tbsp vegetable oil

1tbsp grated fresh ginger

1tsp ground cinnamon

1tsp cumin seeds

½tsp turmeric

2 onions, chopped

2 cups/440g canned red kidney beans, rinsed and drained

2 cups/440g canned soy beans, rinsed and drained

2 cups/440g canned chickpeas rinsed and drained

1¾ cups/375g chopped cooked chicken (optional)

2 cups/440g canned tomato paste

1 cup/250ml vegetable stock

⅓ cup/75g currants

2tbsp pinenuts

Moroccan Beans

Method

Preheat the oven. Heat the oil in a flame and oven-proof casserole dish. Add the onions, garlic, chilies, cumin and cilantro and then gently fry for 1-2 minutes to release their flavors.

Stir in the potatoes, lemon zest and juice to taste, then add the bouillon and seasoning. Bring to the boil, cover, then cook in the oven for 40 minutes, or until the vegetables are tender and the liquid has reduced slightly.

Transfer to plates and top each serving with a spoonful of the sour cream. Sprinkle over the parsley to garnish.

Ingredients

3tbsp olive oil

2 onions, sliced

3 cloves garlic, chopped

2 red chilies, finely chopped

1tsp ground cumin

1tsp ground cilantro

2lb/900g waxy potatoes, cut into ¼in/5mm thick slices

grated zest of 1 lemon, and juice of 1-2 lemons

4 cups/960ml vegetable bouillon

salt and black pepper

4tbsp sour cream to serve

3tbsp chopped fresh parsley to garnish

Moroccan Potato and Lemon Casserole

Method

Heat the oil in a large saucepan. Add the onion, chilli, garlic and ginger and cook for 5 minutes or until softened, stirring occasionally. Stir in the flour, coriander, cumin and turmeric and cook gently, stirring, for 1 minute to release the flavors.

Gradually stir in the stock, then add the passata, cubed root vegetables and the carrots, season with black pepper and mix well.

Bring to the boil, stirring, then cover, reduce the heat and simmer for 45 minutes or until the vegetables are tender, stirring occasionally. Garnish with fresh coriander.

Root Vegetable Curry

Ingredients

1tbsp olive oil

1 onion, chopped

1 green chilli, deseeded and finely chopped

1 clove garlic, finely chopped

1in/2.5cm piece fresh root ginger, finely chopped

2tbsp plain flour

2tsp each ground coriander, ground cumin and turmeric

1½ cups/300ml vegetable stock

1 cup/200ml passata

3 cups/750g mixed root vegetables, such as potato, sweet potato, celeriac and swede, cubed

2 carrots, thinly sliced

Black pepper

Chopped fresh coriander to garnish

Method

Mix together the four spices, black pepper and oil.

Slice the onions into ¼inch/2cm slices. Brush slices each side with the spice mix and place in a greased shallow ovenproof pie plate or flan dish, 10 inches/23cm in diameter, overlapping the slices. Pour over any remaining marinade and add the water to the dish. Cover with foil, sealing the rim well.

Place centre shelf in a preheated oven 350°F/180°C for 25 minutes; the onions will steam and soften. Remove foil, sprinkle with 1 tablespoon sugar and continue to cook uncovered for 20 minutes on top shelf of oven until caramelised.

Spiced Caramelized Onions (Mezgaldi)

Ingredients

1 tsp ground ginger

1 tsp ground cinnamon

¼tsp saffron powder

½tsp turmeric

1 tsp coarse black pepper

2 tbsp olive oil

6 medium onions, peeled

2 tbsp water

1 tbsp sugar

extra sugar

For further garnishing, heat 1 tbsp of sugar in a small pan until it liquifies and turns amber in color. Drizzle over surface of onions. It will set like toffee and give a nice crunch. Serve as an interesting accompaniment.

moroccan

Method

Place the tomatoes in a bowl and cover with boiling water. Leave for 30 seconds, then peel and roughly chop.

Melt the butter in a large saucepan and fry the onion, carrots, celery, pumpkin or swede and pepper for 3-4 minutes, stirring, until softened. Add the chilli and tomatoes, cover and cook for 5 minutes, shaking the pan occasionally. Add the stock, cover and simmer for 20 minutes or until all the vegetables are tender.

Meanwhile, prepare the couscous according to the packet instructions. Stir the chickpeas or broad beans into the vegetables, season, then simmer for 5 minutes or until warmed through. Serve the vegetables piled on top of the couscous.

Spicy Vegetable Couscous

Ingredients

3 plum tomatoes

2tbsp butter

1 large onion, sliced lengthways

2 carrots, cut in half lengthways,

then sliced diagonally

2 sticks celery, sliced

1 cup/300g pumpkin, deseeded, or swede,

cut into 1in/2cm cubes

1 green pepper, deseeded and chopped

1tsp dried crushed chillies

1 cup/300ml vegetable stock;

2 cups/400g couscous

2 cups/400g can chickpeas or broad

beans, drained

Salt and black pepper

Method

Trim ends off the zucchini. Cut in half lengthwise and cut each half into 3 or 4 sticks. They may be halved again if too long.

Heat 2 tablespoons of the oil in a large saucepan, add onion and fry 3 minutes. Add garlic and spices and stir for 30 seconds. Add the zucchini, salt, water and preserved lemon and the remaining oil if needed. Toss to coat with spices and cook over a medium heat for 15 minutes.

Add the chopped parsley and coriander and continue to cook until zucchini is tender about 10-15 minutes. Remove from heat and pour in the lemon juice. Mix together by tossing. Transfer to a serving dish, garnish with preserved lemon strips. Serve as an accompaniment.

Zucchini with Chermoula

Ingredients

2lb/1kg zucchini, washed

preserved lemon strips for garnish

Chermoula

3tbsp olive oil

1 Spanish onion, finely chopped

2 large cloves garlic, finely chopped

¼tsp cayenne pepper

¼tsp cracked black pepper

½tsp paprika

½tsp cumin

½tsp salt

3tbsp lemon juice

⅓ cup/80 ml water

2tsp finely chopped preserved lemon

3tbsp chopped continental parsley

3tbsp chopped fresh coriander

Method

Place almond meal in a bowl and sift in the icing sugar. Add the beaten egg white, almond essence and orange flower or rose water and mix into a firm pliable paste. Pat out into an even shape and cut into 3 even pieces.

Sprinkle work surface with icing sugar and roll 1 piece into a long sausage shape. Pinch along the 'sausage' to extend it to 18 inches/45cm long and ½inch/1cm thick. Repeat with the 2 remaining pieces. Line an 8 inch/20cm round cake pan or flan pan with baking paper.

Place a sheet of filo on work surface, long side in front of you and brush with warm clarified butter. Place a second sheet on top and brush with butter. Place 1 almond strip 2inches/5cm in from edge, fold filo over the almond roll and roll to the end, brush with butter, then form a coil and place in the center of the prepared pan. Form 2 more filo almond rolls and continue the coil. Brush with egg yolk beaten with a little water and place in preheated oven. Bake for 30 minutes.

Remove from oven, place on an oven tray, remove paper and return to oven for 10-15 minutes until golden and crisp. Invert onto a wire rack to cool slightly. Slide onto a serving plate. Sieve icing sugar on the top and sprinkle cinnamon around edge to form a border. Cut into wedges to serve.

Almond Serpent Cake (M'hanncha)

Ingredients

Almond Paste

1 cup/200g almond meal (or ½ cup/210g

packets almond meal)

½ cup/100g icing sugar

1 egg white, lightly beaten

2tsp grated lemon rind

¼tsp almond essence

1tbsp orange flower or rose water

Pastry

9 sheets filo pastry

4tbsp unsalted butter, clarified (see below)

1 egg yolk

2tbsp icing sugar

½tsp cinnamon

moroccan

Method

Place the couscous in a large microwave safe bowl. Add sugar, salt and water and stand until sugar is absorbed. Place in the microwave and cook as directed on page 6. Microwave couscous, adding 6 tablespoons of butter.

On completion, remove from microwave, fluff up and fork through the fruit and almonds.

Pile into a suitable serving dish or platter into a conical shape. If desired, sprinkle the pistachio nuts at the top.

Combine sugar and cinnamon together and serve in a bowl at the table with a jug of hot milk. Each person helps themselves, spooning the couscous into individual bowls.

Ingredients

1 cup/250g instant couscous

¼ cup/56g castor sugar

1 cup hot water

pinch salt

6tbsp unsalted butter, cut into dice

½ cup/112.5g dried apricots, cut into thin strips

4-5 pitted dates, quartered lengthwise

1-2tbsp raisins or sultanas

3-4tbsp blanched almonds, toasted

2tbsp coarsely chopped pistachio nuts, optional

For Serving

2tbsp castor sugar

½tsp cinnamon

1½ cups/350ml hot milk

Sweet Couscous with Nuts and Dried Fruits

Note:

This is usually served as a snack at any time. It also
makes a tasty breakfast dish. Covered leftovers
may be stored in the refrigerator and heated
in the microwave. Other combinations of dried
fruits and nuts may also be used.

moroccan

Method

Whisk the eggs, orange juice and oil together. Add the orange rind and sugar and whisk well.

Sift flour and baking powder together, stir into the egg mixture with a wooden spoon until thoroughly combined.

Sprinkle work surface with extra flour, turn out the dough. Knead lightly until smooth and roll out to ¼inch/½cm thickness. Cut into round cakes with a 2½inch/5cm biscuit cutter.

Place syrup ingredients in a saucepan, stir while it comes to the boil, turn down heat and simmer for 5-6 minutes. Set aside.

Heat deep oil to 17°/340°F or until a ½inch/1cm cube of bread turns golden in 20 seconds. Add honey cakes a few at a time and fry until puffed and golden on both sides. Remove and drain on absorbent paper.

Place a few cakes at a time into the warm syrup, turn to coat then remove to a serving dish with a slotted spoon. Serve immediately.

Deep Fried Honey Puffs

Ingredients

3 eggs

¼ cup/60ml orange juice

¼ cup/60ml vegetable oil

1tbsp grated orange rind

¼ cup/60ml castor sugar

1 cup/300g plain flour

3tbsp extra flour for rolling

vegetable oil for deep frying

1tsp of baking powder

Syrup

2tbsp lemon juice

1½ cups/337g sugar

1½ cups/350ml water; ⅓ cup/80ml honey

1tbsp grated orange rind

Method

Mix the beaten eggs, the granulated sugar, the yeast and the zest of lemon in a container. Add the chopped almonds and the semolina little by little. Work this mixture energetically until the dough is soft.

Dampen the hands with the water of orange blossom, remove thick part like a walnut of dough, make a ball of it and flatten it very slightly.

Sprinkle icing sugar on a bench and place the flattened sides of the dough on the sugar. Arrange the balls on a greased baking tray with the sugary side on top.

Cook in an oven set at 200°/400°F for 20-25 minutes. Remove from oven and allow to cool before storing in an air-tight container.

Ghoriba with Almonds

Ingredients

7 beaten eggs

1 cup/250g granulated sugar

1½tsp yeast

zest 1 lemon

1kg/2lb chopped almonds

1 cup/200g semolina

water of orange blossom

icing sugar

Method

Rinse out the tea pot with boiling water. Add tea leaves, sugar and mint leaves.

Pour in the boiling water from a height to oxygenate the water. Place on the lid and stand to infuse for 3-4 minutes. Serve immediately.

Mint Tea (Etzai)

Ingredients

1tbsp Chinese green tea

4tbsp sugar

½ cup/112.5g fresh mint leaves

3 cups/710ml boiling water

Note:

It is traditional to serve the mint tea in glasses.

Garnish with a fresh mint sprig.

Method

Peel oranges. Cut into thin, round slices with a sharp knife. Place on a platter in overlapping circles.

Remove the stones from the dates and slice thinly lengthwise.

Sprinkle on the orange slices and drizzle water all over the orange flower.

Dust with cinnamon passed through a fine strainer. Chill before serving.

Garnish with a fresh mint sprig. Serve with whipped cream or yoghurt.

Ingredients

6 oranges

12 fresh dates

1-2tsp orange flower water

1tsp ground cinnamon

whipped cream or thick yoghurt for serving

Orange and Date Dessert Salad

Method

Cut 4 bananas (peeled) in ½in/1cm slices and place in a bowl. Add apricot liqueur and marinate for half an hour.

In another bowl, place 1 cup/240ml pancake mix while following package directions to make thick pancake batter, using the above liqueur drained from the bananas as part of the liquid.

Add bananas to the batter and stir thoroughly. In a large, heavy-based frying pan, add ½in/1cm worth of cooking oil. Drop the mixture by tablespoonfuls (2 or 3 pieces of banana in each spoon) into the hot fat until golden brown on both sides. Remove and set aside.

Combine ½ cup/112.5g soft bread crumbs, melted butter, sugar and ground ginger. Place pancakes on dessert plates and sprinkle 1 to 2 tbsp breadcrumb mixture on the pancakes.

Ingredients

4 bananas

½ cup/120ml apricot liqueur

1 cup/240ml pancake mix

vegetable oil for frying

½ cup/112.5g soft bread crumbs (grated fresh bread)

3 tbsp melted butter

4tbsp sugar

1tsp ground ginger

Peasant Pancakes

Note:

Crystallised ginger may be used instead of ground

ginger, in which case, use 2 tbsp sugar and 2 tbsp

crystallised ginger, minced finely.

moroccan

Index